WILD
DISCOVERIES
WACKY NEW
ANIMALS

BY HEATHER L.
MONTGOMERY

Scholastic Inc.

Jason Brown, center right inset: Courtesy Jason Brown, bottom right: Courtesy Jason Brown, bottom left: Courtesy Evan Twomey; pages 14–15: Courtesy Geoff Gallice/Wikimedia; page 14 inset: John Downer/Nature Picture Library; page 15 inset: Courtesy Bernal Morera and Julian Monge-Najera/Tropinature.com; pages 16–17 (all): Cassius V. Stevani/IQ-USP, Brazil; page 18: Piotr Naskrecki/Minden Pictures; page 19: Bill Curtsinger/National Geographic Stock; page 20–21: David Hall/Seaphotos; page 21 top left inset: Rodger Klein/WaterFrame/ Biosphoto, top center inset: Birgitte Wilms/Minden Pictures, top right inset: Birgitte Wilms/Getty Images; pages 22–23: K.J. Osborn/ National Museum of Natural History, Smithsonian Institution; page 23 top left inset: K.J. Osborn/National Museum of Natural History, Smithsonian Institution, bottom right inset: Greg Pio/Courtesy MBARI; pages 24–25: Courtesy Marijke Wilhelmaus; page 24 top left inset: Courtesy Dr. Allen Collins, Tara Lynne and the Smithsonian National Museum of Natural History, bottom left: Ned DeLoach/fishid. com; pages 26–27: Greg Rouse; page 27 inset: Greg Rouse; page 28: Richard Smith/Ocean Realm Images; page 29: Gardel Bertrand/Getty Images; pages 30–31 Geoff Deehan; page 30 inset: Geoff Deehan; page 31 inset: Carsten Peter/National Geographic Stock; pages 32–33: Luc Novovitch/Getty Images; page 33 bottom left: Courtesy Henrik Krehenwinkel; page 34 (all): Courtesy Patrick Schmitz, Rubinoff Lab, University of Hawaii; page 35: Courtesy Samuel W. James, University of Iowa; pages 36–37 (all): Courtesy Dr. Frank Glaw; page 38: John D. McHugh/AP Photo; page 39: Ingmar Wesemann/Getty Images; pages 40–41: Alejandro Arteaga Nature Photography; page 41 inset: Alejandro Arteaga Nature Photography; pages 42–43: Courtesy Dr. Francesco Rovero; page 44: Dr. Tim Davenport/WCS; page 45 background: Jeremy Holden/Courtesy Fauna & Flora International, inset photos: Courtesy BANCA/PRCF/Flora & Fauna International; pages 46–47: Tim Laman/Nature Picture Library; page 47 bottom left: Courtesy Dr. Marcel Holyoak/UC Davis, bottom center left: Bruce Beehler/ NHPA/Photoshot, bottom center: Tim Laman/naturepl.com, bottom center right: Michele Westmoreland/Animals Animals Enterprises, right: Courtesy Dr. Marcel Holyoak/UC Davis; page 48: Courtesy Andrew Richards/Bohart Museum of Entomology; page 49 background: Badboo/Dreamstime.com, top left inset: Visions of America/Superstock, center top: Piotr Naskrecki/Minden Pictures, top right inset: Joshua Haviv/Shutterstock, bottom right: Jason Gibbs, bottom center inset: Courtesy Dr. William M. Moe, bottom left inset: Hemera Technologies/Getty Images; pages 50–51 background: Courtesy Todd W. Pierson, bottom filmstrip photos: Courtesy Dr. Stephen M. Deban; page 51 bottom right inset: Bill Peterman; pages 52–53: Courtesy Guenter A. Schuster; page 52 inset: Carl E. Williams/Tennessee Wildlife Resources Agency; page 53 inset: De Agostini Picture Library/Getty Images; page 54 left: Courtesy Mark Colyn, right: Courtesy Yann Le Bris; page 55: Dr. David Phillips/Visuals Unlimited, Inc.; pages 56–57 background: Thaikrit/Shutterstock; page 56: Courtesy Dr. John La Salle; page 57 top left inset: Courtesy Gevork Arakalian, Ph.D., top right inset: Courtesy Dr. Gevork Arakalian, bottom left: Planetary Visions; page 58 background: Surawach5/Shutterstock, top: iStockphoto/Thinkstock, left: Brand X Pictures/Thinkstock, right: Ryan McVay/Thinkstock; page 59 background: Courtesy Dr. Anne Fawcett, inset: Courtesy Dr. Mark E. Siddal; pages 60–61 (all): Courtesy Paul Valentich-Scott/Santa Barbara Museum of Natural History; page 63: Dorling Kindersley/Getty Images; page 64: Simonlong/Flikr/Getty Images.

ISBN 978-0-545-47767-3

Text copyright © 2013 by Heather L. Montgomery.

All rights reserved. Published by Scholastic Inc.
SCHOLASTIC and associated logos are trademarks and/or registered trademarks of Scholastic Inc.

12 11 10 9 8 7 6 5 4 3 2 1   13 14 15 16 17 18/0

Printed in the U.S.A.   40
First Scholastic printing, January 2013
Designed by Liz Herzog
Photo research by Alan Gottlieb

TABLE OF CONTENTS

Letter to the Reader 4
Discovery 101 5
Name Games 6

RAIN FORESTS 7
Shocking Pink Dragon Millipede 8
Caquetá Titi Monkey 10
Blessed Poison Frog 12
Giant Velvet Worm 14
Little Star Mushroom 16
Atewa Hooded Spider 18

OCEANS 19
Psychedelic Frogfish 20
Green Bomber 22
Bonaire Banded Box Jelly 24
Rosy Boneworm 26
Satomi's Pygmy Seahorse 28

ISLANDS 29
Siau Island Tarsier 30
Giant Whip Scorpion 32
Amphibious Caterpillar 34
Blue Earthworm 35
Timon's Chameleon 36
Chan's Megastick 38

MOUNTAINS 39
Condor Glassfrog 40
Gray-Faced Sengi 42
Matilda's Horned Viper 44
Burmese Snub-Nosed Monkey 45
Wattled Smoky Honeyeater 46
Black Warrior Wasp 48

WACKY PLACES 49
Patch-Nosed Salamander 50
Tennessee Bottlebrush Crayfish 52
Walter's Duiker 54
Histicola Bacteria 55
Blue Gum Gall Wasp 56

KIDS IN ACTION 58
T. Rex Leech 59
Isabella's Bittersweet Clam 60

Glossary 62
About the Author 64

Dear Explorer,

Scientists have identified almost one million different animals creeping, peeking, and sneaking across this earth! That number blows my mind! When I realized there may be as many as six million (new) ones still waiting to be discovered—and that they are all a bit wacky—I couldn't wait to write this book!

The animals I've included were officially described between 2007 and 2012. I've also slipped in a few special cases—little star mushroom and histicola bacteria aren't animals. They are just so cool I couldn't leave them out.

I've highlighted places (like rain forests) where many discoveries are being made. New animals are found in other places, too; I simply couldn't fit them all!

You'll find basic facts about each animal listed in the sidebar on each page. These facts include the animal's "scientific name" and its "role in nature." An animal's "role in nature" is basically that animal's job, such as being a carnivore in the food chain.

Get reading already! I need help on the search for new wild discoveries!

Heather L. Montgomery

NOT NEW? Not a single creature in this book is "new" to the earth. In fact, most of them have been around longer than humans! But every one of them is new to science.

Animals are discovered all across the planet, by people who speak different languages and have different ideas about animals. But scientists, no matter where they are from, treat discoveries in a similar way. Every new type of creature discovered is a new "species." A species is a group of animals that are all the same kind. For example, all bald eagles are the same species. Bald eagles are all similar in size, coloring, and behavior—but they are different from other birds such as American robins. Each species of animal has special traits.

DISCOVERY 101

HIGH-TECH TOYS

Thanks to advanced technology, **AMAZING ANIMAL DISCOVERIES HAPPEN EVERY DAY.** Explorers can view the earth from a satellite, check an animal's DNA bar code, or even use a robotic submarine to uncover new animals. Believe it or not, people are discovering as many as two life-forms per hour!

MOSTLY SPINELESS

Only 3% of recently discovered species have backbones—these include animals like antelopes and monkeys. Most new discoveries are of **CREATURES WITHOUT BACKBONES,** such as insects, worms, and clams. The rest are of plants, fungi, and microscopic life-forms.

RECENTLY DISCOVERED SPECIES

3% are animals with backbones

25% are plants, fungi and microscopic life-forms

72% are animals without backbones

When an animal is discovered, a scientist describes it by writing an article for a scientific journal. In the article, the scientist gets to name the animal. Each animal is given a scientific name, and some are given common names as well.

An animal's scientific name is written in Latin and is understood by scientists around the world (no matter what language they speak). It works like a **SECRET CODE**—each part has a special meaning. For example, the code might describe an unusual trait the animal has. The common name is like a nickname and many animals have more than one.

Some scientists come up with **WACKY** names! Check out these fun ones:

NAME GAMES

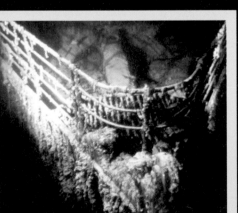

TARZAN CHAMELEON
(common name)
This chameleon climbs trees just like Tarzan, the jungle hero!

SPONGIFORMA SQUAREPANTSII
(scientific name)
Can you guess which cartoon character this fungus is named after?

HALOMONAS TITANICAE
(scientific name)
This bacteria was found eating the steel of the *Titanic*!

PANCAKE BATFISH
(common name)
Flat as a pancake, this fish hops around on its fins!

Tropical rain forests cover only 6% of the earth's surface, but **THEY MAY CONTAIN HALF OF THE SPECIES ON THE PLANET!** Why are there so many types of animals in a rain forest? There are many layers to a rain forest. From branches waving up in the sun to a dark, damp forest floor, each layer offers different food and living conditions. Because of this, each layer is home to different species.

A rain forest also gets over four feet of rain each year! With plenty of water and lots of layers, rain forests bubble over with **ANIMALS TO DISCOVER.** The amazing variety of animals found in the world's rain forests is one reason why it's important for everyone to **HELP PROTECT THEM.**

RAIN FORESTS

8

SHOCKING PINK DRAGON MILLIPEDE

Scientific Name: *Desmoxytes purpurosea*

Size: 1.2 inches   Role in Nature: Decomposer   Discovered in: Thailand

A weird creature has been discovered creeping through the rain forest. Each segment of its body is guarded by sharp, toothlike hooks. Its legs stick out in all directions. And . . . it is hot pink!

CRAZY COLOR

Many millipedes are brown. They camouflage against the dead leaves they eat. Others are black and yellow or red. Until these millipedes were found, no scientist had ever seen a pink one!

Why are dragon millipedes such a crazy color? Is it nature's way of saying that they are dangerous? The color may **WARN PREDATORS** about the sharp spikes or about the possibility of poison.

OUCH!

Millipedes are not very dangerous to people. However, their cousins, the centipedes, can give you a painful bite. To tell them apart, **LOOK AT THEIR FEET** ("pede" means "foot"). Millipedes have two pairs of feet per segment. Centipedes have one pair per segment. Stay away from them!

FOUND!

Shocking pink dragon millipedes have been found in **ONLY ONE PLACE** on the planet —Hup Pa Tard cave in Thailand. Hundreds of them were found crowded on top of wet rocks.

(UN)SOLVED MYSTERY: POISON ALERT?

The dragon millipede is related to a bright-red-and-black millipede, which **OOZES POISON** out of its body. The poison from just one of these millipedes can kill eighteen pigeons! This poison smells like bitter almonds. Dragon millipedes smell like almonds, too. Do they give off poison? In the future, someone will figure out the answer to this question. Perhaps it will be you!

Apheloria

CAQUETÁ TITI MONKEY

Scientific Name: *Callicebus caquetensis*

Size: 13.8 inches Role in Nature: Omnivore Discovered in: Colombia

In 1969, a scientist spotted a cat-sized monkey in the Amazon jungle. The markings on the monkey's face were different from other monkeys', and the scientist became curious about it. Unfortunately, gangs were at war in the region, so no one could go exploring. Scientists wanted to know more about that mysterious monkey!

After thirty years, it was finally safe to explore the area. A different scientist, Javier García, hiked through the rain forest for forty-three days. He listened for the monkey's calls. García found the monkey and proved that it existed!

MONKEY CHAT

Titis make a lot of noise. They

squeak, gobble-gobble-gobble,

TOGETHER ♥ FOREVER

Once a male titi monkey finds a mate, he sticks with her for life. The two monkeys sit side by side on a branch and **WRAP THEIR TAILS TOGETHER.** The couple has one baby each year. The father holds, cares for, and plays with the baby. Like other mammals, the mother feeds the baby her milk. When the baby is old enough, it will eat fruits and insects, like its parents. At night, the family cuddles together in a tree.

Caquetá titi monkey eating guava fruit

achooo,
and even
purrrrr!

BLESSED POISON FROG

Scientific Name: *Ranitomeya benedicta*
Size: 0.75 inches   Role in Nature: Carnivore   Discovered in: Peru

With bright red on their heads and bubbly patterns on their back ends, blessed poison frogs are easy to see. Until recently, though, no one knew they existed. How did these frogs stay hidden for so long? They live on the top floors of the rain forest. Since these guys seldom come down, earthbound people were rarely able to catch a glimpse of them.

SHOW OFF

The poison frog's flashy colors may warn **PREDATORS** to stay away—the frogs pack poison in their skin. Their colorful skin may also attract another frog's attention. Bright colors can help them recognize their friends in the shadows of the rain forest.

Golden poison dart frog

PIGGY BACK

Like other amphibians, these frogs begin their lives as eggs. After the eggs hatch on the forest floor, the tadpoles' parents haul them high into the trees on their backs. There, the parents give them **WHAT ALL KIDS WANT**— their own swimming pools! Each nursery is a pool of water caught in plant leaves and full of food.

SHHH!

The scientists who found this little frog were tempted to keep it a secret. Smugglers search out colorful frogs and **SELL THEM AS PETS.** Because there were only a few blessed poison frogs found, scientists did not want **SMUGGLERS** to get their hands on them. In the end, the scientists told their secret because they felt it was their duty to tell the world about their discovery.

SIZE: 0.75 INCHES!

EYE SPY

Unlike most other frogs, blessed poison frogs have **EXCEPTIONAL EYESIGHT** and are adapted to be active during the day.

UNSOLVED MYSTERY: NO BRIDGES

Blessed poison frogs live in a forest bordered by rivers. No one yet knows if they can cross the rivers and leave the forest. Perhaps they can't— that would explain why so far they have been found in only one place in the world.

GIANT VELVET WORM

Scientific Name: *Peripatus solorzanoi*

Size: 8.5 inches Role in Nature: Carnivore Discovered in: Costa Rica

A long tube glides across moss on a dark, wet forest floor. It cruises under leaves and over rotten logs on soft, stumpy legs. When its long feeler touches a cricket, the worm rears back. It shoots a web of slime. The giant velvet worm has caught its next meal.

SUPER SNOT

A velvet worm **SQUIRTS SLIMY GLUE** from two spray guns under its head. As the ropes of slime shoot out, the guns swivel from side to side. They weave a web in midair! The prey is trapped under a sticky web in less than a second.

Rare photo of giant velvet worm

UNSOLVED MYSTERY: MAXED OUT?

Velvet worms don't have lungs. Holes in their sides **LET AIR FLOW INTO TUBES** inside their bodies. But air flows in only so far. Scientists wonder if, at 8.5 inches, this guy is as big as a velvet worm can be. Why? If a velvet worm's body were too large, the center parts wouldn't get any oxygen.

PHANTOM WORMS

Giant velvet worms are extremely hard to find. One scientist spent thousands of dollars and several weeks searching and, still, she could not find one. Experts predict that as many as ninety other species of velvet worms remain to be discovered.

SLURP TIME

With extra-sharp teeth, the velvet worm cuts into the prey's body. It injects chemicals that turn the prey's insides into a tasty liquid. **SLURP!** The worm sucks out its meal.

Unidentified velvet worm

On a pitch-black night, Dr. Dennis Desjardin stalked through the jungle. Rustling, crackling, and slithering noises surrounded him. Jaguars and vipers were hunting, too. Yet he switched off his flashlight. He knew the bright beam would cover up the soft light of his prey—glowing mushrooms.

Looking down, he found his treasure. "It was like looking up at the night sky," recalled Dr. Desjardin. He named the glowing mushroom "asterina," which means "little star."

LITTLE STAR MUSHROOM

Scientific Name: *Mycena asterina*

Size: 1 inch **Role in Nature:** Decomposer **Discovered in:** Brazil

NO ANIMALS HERE! MUSHROOMS ARE NOT ANIMALS. THEY ARE FUNGI.

SECRETS OF THE NIGHT

Some mushrooms, like the little star mushroom, glow on their stalk and cap. Others keep their light a secret by only glowing on their hyphae. The white hyphae are the rootlike parts as fine as hair. They normally stay unseen below the soil. When grown in a laboratory, hyphae can look like **SPOOKY EYEBALLS**.

MUSHROOM HUNTER

Hunting mushrooms is not easy. It's not always safe, either. On Dr. Desjardin's expeditions, he has come came **FACE-TO-FACE** with a cobra—and with the large lizard that was chasing that cobra!

USEFUL STUFF!

Glowing mushrooms have been used as lanterns. People have also **SMEARED THE SLIMY GLOW ON THEIR FACES** to scare enemies. Some mushrooms glow less when there are pollutants in the soil. In the future, people may even use those mushrooms to help clean up the earth!

LIGHTING THE WAY

At least seventy different types of mushrooms glow in the dark. And Dr. Desjardin has discovered one-fourth of them! He is lighting up our understanding of these strange fungi. Here are some others he's tracked down.

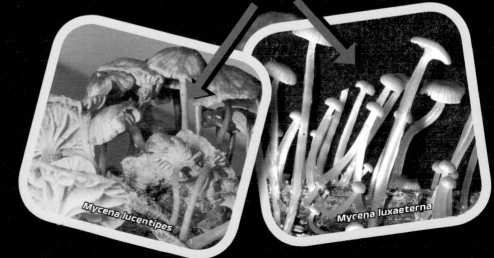

Mycena lucentipes

Mycena luxaeterna

ATEWA HOODED SPIDER

Scientific Name: *Ricinoides atewa*

Size: 0.4 inches Role in Nature: Carnivore Discovered in: Ghana

These eight-legged beasts creep through tunnels in the soil. Even though they are less than half an inch long, Atewa hooded spiders have been nicknamed **"DINOSPIDERS."** They are the largest hooded spiders ever found!

BUT WAIT! I WANT EIGHT!

When hooded spiders hatch, they have six legs. But later on, they grow two more!

UNSOLVED MYSTERY: WHAT DO YOU EAT?

Atewa hooded spiders live among dead leaves, under rocks, and in the tunnels of abandoned termite nests. Scientists know they are predators. But do they dine on bugs that live under the soil, or do they catch creatures on top of the soil? No one knows—yet!

FRANKENSPIDER

The Atewa hooded spider appears to be MADE UP OF PARTS FROM OTHER CREATURES. It has two body segments and eight legs like a spider. Its pincers are mini versions of a scorpion's. And, like a daddy longlegs, its second pair of legs work like feelers. This spider has something unique, though: a built-in hood that's good for cover in sun or rain.

Oceans make up 71% of the earth's surface and they are swimming with species waiting to be identified. **MILLIONS OF OCEAN CREATURES HAVE NEVER EVEN BEEN SEEN BY A HUMAN EYE.** Those creatures hide thousands of feet below the surface of the ocean. They blend into the dark, deep waters. They thrive in the cold depths of the ocean where **NO HUMAN COULD SURVIVE.**

But scientists and other curious people don't give up easily. Scuba gear, underwater cameras, and submarines with robotic arms are all put to use to expose the wacky animals hiding in the sea.

OCEANS

PSYCHEDELIC FROGFISH

Scientific Name: *Histiophryne psychedelica*

Size: 4 inches **Role in Nature:** Carnivore **Discovered in:** Ambon Bay, Indonesia

In the waters of Indonesia, a scuba diver spots a fish that seems to have come right out of a dream. Peach and white ribbons of color stretch out from the rims of its turquoise eyes. Meet the psychedelic frogfish!

HIDE AND SEEK

The eye-catching swirls on the frogfish's colorful skin appear to be a poor attempt at **CAMOUFLAGE**—until the fish nestles among coral that has a similar pattern. Then, the psychedelic frogfish blends right in with its surroundings.

Just like you are the only person with *your* **FINGERPRINT** pattern, each frogfish has its own set of stripes. If the fish to the left committed a crime . . . could you pick it out of this lineup?

fish number one

fish number two

fish number three

ANSWER: fish number two

UNSOLVED MYSTERY: KILLER CHEEKS?!

Many fish hide inside holes in coral. They get into the holes by backing down into them. When a psychedelic frogfish enters a hole, though, it goes in face-first. It actually chooses a hole that's so small it has to push its way in. Why? Scientists think it may use its flabby face to fill the entrance to the hole—**TRAPPING OTHER ANIMALS INSIDE** for dinner!

HOPPING FROG

A psychedelic frogfish rarely swims. Instead, it hops! Its **GILLS WORK LIKE A JET ENGINE**—the gills squirt water out the back of the fish, shooting the fish forward. The fish pushes off and lands on its fleshy fins as if they were feet.

GREEN BOMBER

GREEN BOMBER

Scientific Name: *Swima bombiviridis* **Size:** 2 inches
Role in Nature: Carnivore **Discovered in:** Pacific Ocean

In the darkest depths of the ocean, a swarm of worms paddles. Oar-like hairs wave along their sides, moving them up, up, up. These aren't any ordinary worms. These worms drop bomb-like sacks. And the sacks glow in the dark!

WHAT'S IN A NAME?

Can you guess what *Swima bombiviridis* means? Use the words hidden within the green bomber's scientific name to figure it out.

READY, AIM, FIRE!

The **"BOMBS"** are actually the gills of the green bomber worms. Eight balloon-like gills hang behind the worm's head. When a predator swims near, the worm casts off a gill and lets it sink into the dark. The gill glows an eerie green. It is harmless, but the predator is lured toward the light. Instead of a worm for supper, all it gets is the worm's **GLOWING** gill. Later, the green bomber worm regrows its gills, ready to bomb again!

ROBOTIC EXPLORER

A mile's worth of water is very heavy! It creates enough pressure to physically crush a human's body. **ROBOTIC SUBMARINES** enable humans to explore the deepest parts of the ocean by **REMOTE CONTROL.** Scientists at the Monterey Bay Aquarium Research Institute used the *Tiburon* sub to discover the green bombers.

> **ANSWER:**
"Swima" describes how this worm moves. "Bombi" has to do with the bombs. "Viridis" means green.

BONAIRE BANDED BOX JELLY

Scientific Name: Tamoya ohboya Size: 2.5 inches (plus 7 inches of tentacle)
Role in Nature: Carnivore Discovered in: Caribbean Sea off the coast of Bonaire

CONTAINER SHAFT THREAD SPINES

STINGERS!

Jellyfish have thousands of miniature stingers on the surface of their tentacles. Each stinger looks like a needle and thread. When the stinger is triggered, the thread explodes out of its container, carrying **VENOM** with it. The stingers are used to paralyze prey and protect the jellyfish. The Bonaire banded box jelly has an extremely painful sting—toxic enough to **SEND VICTIMS TO THE EMERGENCY ROOM!**

THE WINNER IS . . .

The research team held a contest on the Internet to name this creature. Out of seven hundred entries, the scientific name *ohboya* was picked. Can you guess how someone came up with that? A science teacher had thought people would shout **"OH BOY!"** when they saw the Bonaire banded box jelly!

BIG HEAD

The Bonaire banded box jelly is pretty much a see-through sack of water. Inside that bell-shaped sack are a mouth, a gut, four balance organs, and twenty-four eyes!

A team of scientists and others spent **OVER NINE YEARS** working to describe and name this new jellyfish.

2001 — A tourist named Vicki Carr spotted a **STRANGE** jellyfish. It swam like other jellyfish, but it moved faster. Carr was curious, so she took a video. A science teacher named Bud Gillan watched Carr's video. He became **CURIOUS,** too. Over the next ten years, Gillan gathered fifty-one reports of sightings.

2006 — Scientists at the Smithsonian Institute wanted to find out more about this strange jellyfish. But they didn't have an animal to study.

2008 — A scuba diver caught two of these jellyfish for the scientists to study. Unfortunately, one got **LOST IN THE MAIL.**

2008-2010 — Scientists studied every detail of the first specimen. The team worked with Gillan to prepare a paper about the new species.

2010 — The lost specimen was **FOUND!** With the help of two Brazilian scientists and a third specimen, Gillan and the scientists were able to finish their paper.

2011 — The **BONAIRE BANDED BOX JELLY** became official!

RoSy BoneWoRM

Scientific Name: *Osedax roseus* **Size:** 2.75 inches (with palps)

Role in Nature: Decomposer **Discovered in:** Monterey Bay, California

For animals that live on the ocean floor, food can be hard to find. When a whale dies, though, gravity brings a ton—actually up to one hundred fifty tons—of food to the creatures in the ocean's basement. Fish, lobster, and sea cucumbers pig out until nothing's left but bones. That's when the rosy boneworms move in! They eat the bones of dead whales and other animals.

A WHALE OF A MEAL

One dead whale feeds up to thirty thousand creatures! In addition to boneworms, over four hundred other types of animals depend on dead whale bodies for food.

PALPS

TRUNK

ROOTS

A boneworm's body has three main parts: roots, trunk, and palps. The roots reach down into the bone, where the food is. The trunk can bend or shrink and is surrounded by a jellylike tube. The feathery palps **DANCE IN THE CURRENT,** collecting oxygen so the boneworm can breathe in its underwater habitat.

These worms depend on bacteria to digest their food for them. Bacteria live on the worm's roots. They turn the bones into food the worms can use.

SNOT FLOWER

Boneworms have been called "snot flowers" because the tube-shaped part of their body is **CLEAR LIKE SNOT.** But when their frilly red palps spread out in the water, boneworms look like dainty flowers.

MINI MEN

Male boneworms are so small they are practically invisible! And up to fourteen males actually live inside a female boneworm's jellylike tube!

SATOMI'S PYGMY SEAHORSE

Scientific Name: *Hippocampus satomiae*

Size: 0.5 inches **Role in Nature:** Carnivore **Discovered in:** Celebes Sea, Indonesia

In the warm waters off of Indonesia, a miniature, S-shaped fish vanishes among the sea fans. Is this a fish with an invisibility cloak? No! It is Satomi's pygmy seahorse. And its camouflage is just about perfect. This seahorse's body is covered in crusty spines that match the color and shape of the sea fans to which it clings.

SUCKING SNOUT

When prey comes within striking range, this seahorse aims its snout toward the food. **SLURP!** The pointy snout sucks the food in like a vacuum, whooshing it right down into the seahorse's intestines.

ACTUAL SIZE!

MR. M♥M

Female pygmy seahorses don't have babies; the males do. A daddy pygmy seahorse carries the seahorse eggs in a pouch on his front. When the eggs hatch, jet-black babies the size of a comma on this page come out. **HELLO, WORLD!**

There are thousands upon thousands of islands on earth. Some of **THE WACKIEST CREATURES LIVE ON ISLANDS.** This is because each island has a unique combination of climate, land forms, and natural resources. Animals that live on an island must be adapted to that island's unique environment.

For example, on the Hawaiian Islands, streams rush down the steep sides of ancient volcanoes. Some animals are adapted to take advantage of those fast-running streams. The island of Barbados doesn't have a single volcano or mountain on it. The soil there is made from ancient shells and coral. The creatures that are adapted to Hawaii's fast-running water wouldn't survive on the island of Barbados.

See? Every island has its own set of conditions, **IDEAL FOR EXTREME ANIMALS!**

ISLANDS

SIAU ISLAND TARSIER

Scientific Name: *Tarsius tumpara*

Size: 5 inches **Role in Nature:** Carnivore **Discovered in:** Indonesia

On a tiny island, a ball of fur clings to the trunk of a tree. As cute as a teddy bear, as weird as an alien, this fluffy creature is one of the most endangered primates on the planet! It is a Siau Island tarsier.

LEAPING LEGS

Extra-long hind legs let the tarsier leap through the air. Some species of tarsiers can leap more than **FIFTEEN TIMES THEIR BODY LENGTH.** If you could do that, you could jump over nine beds lined up end to end!

A tarsier grips a tree's bark with toe pads and props itself up with a superlong tail. Its tail is about twice as long as its body!

VIOLENT VOLCANO

Siau Island tarsiers live only on Siau Island. They cannot be found anywhere else in the world! A volcano has claimed the northern half of this island. On March 11, 2011, it **BELCHED SMOKE AND SPEWED LAVA.** This may be why these wide-eyed cuties all huddle on the southern-most tip of the island.

NIGHT HUNTER

Siau Island tarsiers are nocturnal. They hunt insects and small animals at night using these special adaptations:

SWIVEL TOP: Tarsiers can twist their heads 180° in each direction to pinpoint their prey.

ALL EYES: Tarsiers' eyes are huge. Each eyeball is larger than the animal's brain!

POUNCING PREDATOR: A tarsier can swoop down on prey and snatch it—even in midair.

GIANT WHIP SCORPION

Scientific Name: Thelyphonoides panayensis

Size: 2 inches (including claws) Role in Nature: Carnivore Discovered in: Philippines

A two-inch body size may not sound threatening, but the giant whip scorpion is a real monster. To start with, it has robot-like claws, a long lashing tail, and a secret weapon!

PREPARED FOR BATTLE

The whip scorpion's body is covered with thick plates of armor. It holds up huge pincers, prepared to crush its prey. Its tail flops forward like a deadly whip. And an acid spray gun is loaded and ready. **WATCH OUT!**

Giant whip scorpions have the body and claws of a true scorpion, but they lack the scorpion's powerful sting. They can't make venom. With eight legs plus two body parts, giant whip scorpions seem spiderlike. But, they can't spin silk. So **WHAT ARE THESE LITTLE MONSTERS?** They are relatives of spiders, scorpions, and even horseshoe crabs. Whip scorpions are in a group all their own, though—because of their unique body parts.

A related whip scorpion, *Mastigoproctus giganteus*, found in the United States

TERRIBLE TAIL

Surprisingly, the whip scorpion's tail is only used as a feeler. But at the base of its tail, a whip scorpion hides two sacs filled with acid. When threatened, the animal arches its back, waves its tail overhead, and **SHOOTS THE ENEMY** with the acid from these sacs. The acid spray fights off predators like lizards, armadillos, and even armies of ants. The acid is not deadly, but if you were to get sprayed, you'd have burning eyes and itchy skin!

Actual giant whip scorpion

A TOAD'S LUNCH

When giant whip scorpions were being first studied, four of them were found in bits and pieces inside a toad's stomach. **CROAK!**

NO SCUBA GEAR NEEDED

At the edge of a creek, a yellow caterpillar climbs on dry rocks. When rain pours down, the creek floods. The caterpillar spins a line of silk and anchors itself to a rock. **WATER SWIRLS OVER THE CATERPILLAR.** No problem. To breathe, it takes in oxygen right through its skin!

AMPHIBIOUS CATERPILLAR

Scientific Name: *Hyposmocoma kahamanoa*
Size: 0.2 inches
Role in Nature: Herbivore
Discovered in: Hawaii

Amphibious caterpillars are insects with a superpower no other caterpillars have. Like true amphibians, amphibious caterpillars can hang out on land or underwater!

MOBILE HOME

An amphibious caterpillar builds a home, called a case, which it carries on its back. To make this home, the caterpillar uses silver silk, which it spins, plus sand, lichen, and algae.

ALL GROWN UP

Amphibious caterpillars grow up to become moths. Once they turn into moths, they **TRADE IN THEIR UNDERWATER ABILITIES FOR THEIR WINGS.**

Amphibious caterpillar in its moth state

BLUE EARTHWORM

Size: 9 inches **Role in Nature:** Decomposer? **Discovered in:** Philippines

Scientific Name: *Archipheretima middletoni*

TOP 5 WACKY TRAITS

5 It doesn't tunnel underground.

4 When it is young, it lives in a tree.

3 It is covered in yellow polka dots.

2 If you scare one, it will spray you.

1 It's blue!!!

UNSOLVED MYSTERY: DIRT FOR DINNER?

A typical earthworm can eat half of its body weight in dirt each day. What does the blue earthworm eat? Experts have **CHECKED ITS POOP** to figure it out, but they still aren't sure!

Rumor has it that when blue earthworms grow up, they turn into eels. But they don't. They are just really weird.

CRAZY CAMO

Can a blue body and bright spots camouflage this creature? Yes! Under the thick cover of trees, the ground is dark. Sun rays slip through the branches and dot slick, wet leaves with **SPOTS OF LIGHT.** Wait. Is that a spot of light or a spot on a worm?

Picture a lizard that can change colors, swivel its eyes, and coil its tail into the shape of a cinnamon roll. It's a chameleon. Now, add flashy blue dots, an eye that is half blue and half green, plus short horns. You've got a very special reptile—a male Timon's chameleon!

TIMON'S CHAMELEON

Scientific Name: *Furcifer timoni*
Size: 7.7 inches Role in Nature: Carnivore Discovered in: Amber Mountain, Madagascar

GLAM ROCK STARS

WHITE LIPSTICK AND BLUE EYE SHADOW?

Zebra stripes, neon dots, and bright red blush? Timon's chameleons look more like makeup-covered rock stars than lizards! The males' foreheads are decorated with blue and the females' are red, dotted with blue.

WICKED FAST

A chameleon moves extra slow, but its tongue moves extra fast. Its tongue shoots out in a fraction of a second. If you blinked, you'd miss it! The chameleon's **SLIMY TONGUE TIP SPLATS** onto an unsuspecting bug. It grabs on like a suction cup and pulls the bug back to the chameleon's waiting jaws. Bye-bye, bug!

UNSOLVED MYSTERY: COLOR-CODED

Scientists are puzzled by the patterns and changing colors of Timon's chameleon. But they think the chameleons may use their wild colors to communicate. For example, a female's red head could be code for: "Buzz off! I'm taken."

WORLD FAMOUS

The German who discovered this reptile named it for his seven-year-old son, Timon. Would you like to have **A LIZARD NAMED AFTER YOU?**

High in a tree on the island of Borneo, a stick lays hidden. The stick is slowly dropping eggs to the ground, one by one by one. What kind of stick can do this? Chan's megastick— the world's longest insect!

CHAN'S MEGASTICK

Scientific Name: *Phobaeticus chani* Size: 22 inches (with legs extended)
Role in Nature: Herbivore Discovered in: Malaysia

STICK'S TRICKS

There are **THREE THOUSAND DIFFERENT KINDS** of stick insects on earth. Check out these fun stick insect facts:

■ **Some stick insects spray a stinky mist on any animal that attacks them—including humans!**

■ **Stick insects shed their skin as they grow. Some young stick insects eat that dead skin.**

Are these facts true for Chan's megastick? Since **ONLY THREE** have been found so far, we'll have to wait to find out!

ARM'S LENGTH

With legs and all, Chan's megastick is **NEARLY TWO FEET LONG.** That's about as long as your arm!

Mountains cover about 20% of the earth's surface. **THAT'S A LOT OF STEEP LAND FOR ANIMALS TO DEAL WITH!** Mountains present different habitats than flat lands do. Plus, the habitats at the bottom, middle, and top of a mountain are different from one another. Each level varies in temperature, types of plants that grow there, and amount of rain or snow that falls there. Like the layers of the rain forest, each level of a mountain may be home to different types of animals. Those that live at the top may not find their favorite food at the bottom. Because of this, **MOUNTAINS ARE CRAWLING WITH ALL KINDS OF DIFFERENT SPECIES**—many of which are yet to be identified.

MOUNTAINS

CONDOR GLASSFROG

Scientific Name: Centrolene condor

Discovered in: Condor Mountains, Ecuador

Size: 1 inch **Role in Nature:** Carnivore

When the sun sets, Dr. Diego Cisneros-Heredia slips on his headlamp. He heads up a mountain slope. Heavy rubber boots keep him dry as he splashes into a fast-flowing river. Frogs cling to leaves hanging out over the water. The dark hides them until they chirp and give themselves away. With a quick hand and a sure foot, he snags one. A new glassfrog!

A FOREST FOR ELVES?

The Condor glassfrog is endemic to the elfin forest on a mountain in Ecuador. The forest was given the nickname "elfin" because the **TREES ARE SHORT.** The forest is high on the mountain, where strong winds force the trees to grow thicker rather than taller.

SEE-THROUGH

Glassfrogs are named for the clear skin on their bellies. You can **SEE RIGHT THROUGH TO THEIR GUTS!** With another type of glassfrog, the see-through glassfrog, you can even see its red heart beating.

ALL ALONE?

No other glassfrog species live where the Condor glassfrog was found. Other glassfrogs live in nearby mountain ranges, but they are separated from this species by dry valleys and tall mountain slopes.

COMPLETELY CAMO

Not only is this frog's **SKIN** green, but its **BONES** are green, too! Now that's camouflage!

GRAY-FACED SENGI

Scientific Name: *Rhynchocyon udzungwensis*

Size: 22 inches Role in Nature: Carnivore Discovered in: Udzungwa Mountains, Tanzania

In the mountains of Africa, a hidden camera catches pictures of a strange new mammal. It has a nose like an elephant, weighs as much as a guinea pig, and digs for bugs like an armadillo. The high-tech camera has "trapped" a gray-faced sengi in the dense forest.

SLEEP TIGHT

Many small mammals are nocturnal. Not gray-faced sengis. When it gets dark, they **CRAWL INTO A BED** of dry leaves and go to sleep. Each gray-faced sengi has several nests scattered around so it can have its pick each night.

NICKNAMES

Sengis were not always called sengis. They used to be called elephant shrews. This was because of how they look. Their long noses remind people of elephant trunks. And a shrew is a small animal that looks like a mouse. Sengis are in fact distantly **RELATED TO ELEPHANTS.** But they are not closely related to shrews. Their name has since been changed to sengis.

shrew

elephant

HOME SWEET HOME

Gray-faced sengis are endemic to the Udzungwa Mountains. They aren't found anywhere else in the world.

MATILDA'S HORNED VIPER

Scientific Name: *Atheris matildae*

Size: 2 feet **Role in Nature:** Carnivore **Discovered in:** Tanzania

This snake—with horns, hidden fangs, and powerful venom—seems like a killing machine. Why, then, was it named after a five-year-old girl named Matilda?

VIPER LOVER

Dr. Tim Davenport discovered a black viper with bright zigzags on its back and a yellow belly. He kept the snake in an aquarium to study it. **HIS DAUGHTER, MATILDA, STUDIED IT, TOO.** She helped take care of it, so people nicknamed the snake Matilda's viper. The name stuck!

HIGH STAKES

Matilda's horned viper may be **IN DANGER OF BECOMING EXTINCT.** People have cut down many of the trees in its habitat. Also, because they are so beautiful—and wacky-looking—Dr. Davenport worries that snake collectors will trap them and sell them as pets. He has, thus far, kept their exact location a secret.

UNSOLVED MYSTERY: BORN WITH HORNS

A horned viper's "horns" aren't horns at all. They are horn-shaped scales. What are they for? **TO SCARE AWAY PREDATORS?** To shade the viper's eyes? Scientists haven't found the answer, yet.

BURMESE SNUB-NOSED MONKEY

Scientific Name: *Rhinopithecus strykeri* Size: 21.6 inches (without the tail)

Role in Nature: Herbivore Discovered in: Himalayan Mountains, Burma

Example of a camera trap in use

Many new species that are discovered are tiny creatures that simply haven't been noticed yet. Sometimes, though, a large mammal is found. The Burmese snub-nosed monkey is not huge, but it is definitely noticeable! It has thick black fur, a sneezing problem, and a nose that points the wrong way—up instead of down.

Photos taken by a camera trap

ACHOO!

The easiest way to find this monkey is to wait for it to rain. Water runs off its forehead and into its UPTURNED NOSTRILS. The monkey can't hide quietly anymore—because it is sneezing!

WATTLED SMOKY HONEYEATER

Scientific Name: *Melipotes carolae*

Size: 8.5 inches Role in Nature: Herbivore Discovered in: Foja Mountains, New Guinea

Ever since he was seven years old, Dr. Bruce Beehler has been crazy about birds. As an adult, he gets paid to search for new species of birds and other animals. It's a dream come true!

BLUSHING BIRD

Sometimes a wattled smoky honeyeater blushes. When it gets excited, upset, or angry, its wattle turns a deeper red. **DO YOUR CHEEKS DO THAT?**

PURPLE POO

This bird belongs to a group of birds called honeyeaters. Many honeyeaters eat nectar from flowers (which some people call honey). This bird doesn't eat nectar. At first, no one knew what it ate. Then, the bird **POOPED ALL OVER ONE SCIENTIST'S SHIRT!** The purple poo filled with seeds was good evidence that fruit is this bird's favorite food.

MOUNTAINS OF MYSTERY

Dr. Beehler found a mountain in New Guinea that just begged to be explored. There were no cities. No roads. Not even a trail.

What treasures did the mountain hold? Dr. Beehler was determined to find out! His team flew a helicopter to land at the top.

Within the first few hours, one scientist spotted a black bird with a funny red face. Dr. Beehler searched for days until he finally found the bird! It had a flap of skin (called a wattle) hanging down from each cheek, so he named his treasure the wattled smoky honeyeater.

UNSOLVED MYSTERY: XTREME CHALLENGE

The wattled smoky honeyeater is similar to the common smoky honeyeater. Some experts question whether or not the wattled honeyeater is a separate species. **HOW DIFFERENT DO TWO BIRDS HAVE TO BE TO BE CONSIDERED DIFFERENT SPECIES?** Scientists don't always agree on the answer to that question. It is kind of like asking how different two colors have to be. How do you tell the difference between purple and blue?

How do you tell the difference between species of honeyeaters?

BLACK WARRIOR WASP

Scientific Name: *Megalara garuda* **Size:** 2.5 inches

Role in Nature: Carnivore **Discovered in:** Mekongga Mountains, Indonesia

With a supersized body, eyes stretched across its face, and jaws longer than its legs, this insect may look like a cartoon character. But it's real! Say hello to the black warrior wasp. It measures in at more than two inches long!

STING!

Only female wasps sting. A wasp's stinger is the same body part that is used to lay eggs. Since male wasps don't lay eggs, they don't have a stinger. No one has been stung by a black warrior wasp, so we don't know how painful the sting is. **ANY VOLUNTEERS?**

UNSOLVED MYSTERY!

WALK MUCH?

Since no scientist has ever seen them walk, no one's sure how black warrior wasps are able to walk without tripping on those long jaws. Remember, their jaws are longer than their front legs. **MAYBE THEY CAN'T WALK AT ALL!**

Not all animals are found in remote rain forests, wild mountains, or vast oceans. Fascinating creatures can turn up anywhere—even in the most unexpected places.

Check out these examples:

A new type of heel walker, that looks like a pregnant alien, was found at a truck stop.

A new type of bacteria (that smells like garlic!) showed up at a toxic-waste dump.

Plus, a new bee buzzed through a New York City park!

See? You never know where new species will pop up! Read on to check out other animals found in strange places. . . .

WACKY PLACES

Sclerophasma, or heel walker

Dehalogenimonas lykanthroporepellens, or werewolf-repelling bacteria

Lasioglossum gotham, or Gotham bee

PATCH-NOSED SALAMANDER

Scientific Name: *Urspelerpes brucei*
Size: 1 inch Role in Nature: Carnivore Discovered in: a stream in Georgia

In the foothills of the Appalachian Mountains, several scientists headed into the woods to catch salamanders to study. While the group looked for a "better" stream, Bill Peterman decided to look in the ditch-like stream by the side of the road. In the wet leaves beside the stream, Peterman caught a salamander that was new to science! This cute amphibian became known as the patch-nosed salamander.

MINI-MISSILE

How do these salamanders catch quick insects if they have short legs and no lungs? Scientists have studied close relatives of the patch-nosed salamander and found that they have **AN ELASTIC TONGUE!** The salamander's tongue shoots out like a missile, slaps onto its prey, and yanks the food back into its mouth—all in a matter of milliseconds.

GILL FRILL

When it is young and lives in a stream, the patch-nosed salamander uses frilly gills on its neck to breathe. Many adult salamanders use lungs to breathe. Not the patch-nosed salamander! Once it is grown up, this salamander **BREATHES RIGHT THROUGH ITS SKIN!**

ACTUAL SIZE!

TIGHT QUARTERS

The patch-nosed is the smallest salamander in the United States. It is not much bigger than a dime!

TENNESSEE BUTTLEBRUSH CRAYFISH

Scientific Name: *Barbicambarus simmonsi*

Size: 7 inches Role in Nature: Omnivore Discovered in: a photo taken in Tennessee!

Two new types of crayfish are found in the United States each year! When the Tennessee bottlebrush crayfish was first spotted, though, experts ignored it!

Tennessee bottlebrush crayfish

BLUE BLOOD

People have iron in their blood, which makes it red. But **CRAYFISH HAVE COPPER** in their blood. When there is enough oxygen in crayfish blood, the copper makes it look blue.

CLOSE COUSINS

Crayfish look a lot like their cousins—lobsters. Both belong to the group decapoda. "Deca" means "ten" and "poda" means "foot." Guess how many legs they have!

Lobster

THE CASE OF MISTAKEN IDENTITY

Dr. Chris Taylor is a crayfish expert. One day he received a picture of a crayfish with fuzzy antennae. He knew the only crayfish in the world with antennae like that lived in Kentucky. But the picture was taken in Tennessee. Dr. Taylor guessed the crayfish had been accidentally moved.

When a *second* crayfish with fuzzy antennae was caught in Tennessee, though, he knew something was up! Dr. Taylor set off with three other scientists to **SOLVE THIS CRAYFISH MYSTERY.** After hours of searching, the scientists heaved a rock out of a stream and scooped up a real treasure—a totally new type of crayfish. Meet the Tennessee bottlebrush crayfish!

UNSOLVED MYSTERY: HAIR-RAISING

Why is there fuzz on the Tennessee bottlebrush crayfish's antennae? Just like the **HAIR ON YOUR ARM** lets you feel a breeze, a crayfish's fuzz may allow it to sense movements in the water. Or, it may be used for smelling. Scientists aren't sure yet.

WALTER'S DUIKER

Scientific Name: *Philantomba walteri*

Size: 19.7 inches **Role in Nature:** Herbivore **Discovered in:** a market in Benin

"Duiker" is an African word that means "diver." Walter's duiker is an antelope. Is it an antelope that goes scuba diving? No! This shy antelope dives into a hiding place when anyone comes near.

AT THE MARKET

Imagine making a major discovery in your local market. One scientist did! He stumbled upon **A PILE OF SKULLS FOR SALE** in a meat market in western Africa. The pile included a skull from a small mammal that had never before been identified as a separate species. This turned out to be the skull of a Walter's duiker.

OOPS!

In 1968, Walter Verheyen had collected the first example of a Walter's duiker. For more than forty years, that duiker's skull was in a museum with the **WRONG NAME TAG** on it! Later, Walter's son, Erik Verheyen, worked with other researchers to use DNA to set the story straight. He got the DNA from drilling into the teeth of a Walter's duiker skull. Then, he named the duiker after his father.

HISTICOLA BACTERIA

Size: Microscopic Role in Nature: Unknown Discovered in: a human mouth in England

Scientific Name: *Prevotella histicola*

Believe it or not, a new species might be found *inside* of you! The microscopic histicola bacterium was found lurking in someone's gums during a trip to the dentist.

IN THE MILLIONS

Millions upon millions of bacteria live in a single drop of **HUMAN SPIT.** With all the warmth, moisture, and food in your mouth, it is a perfect place for bacteria to party. Up to seven hundred types of bacteria live in a single mouth. About half of those have yet to be named.

UNSOLVED MYSTERY: FRIEND OR FOE?

In your mouth, bacteria can cause **BAD BREATH** and tooth decay. But some bacteria do good things, too. A mouth wouldn't be healthy without bacteria's help! The good bacteria go to war against the bad bacteria. Is the histicola bacterium good or bad? No one knows yet—so you'd better keep brushing!

Mixed oral bacteria, seen through a scanning electron microscope

THAT'S JUST GROSS!

The histicola bacterium usually survives by dissolving the sugars and proteins in spit. To study it, researchers kept it alive using **HORSE BLOOD!**

BLUE GUM GALL WASP

Scientific Name: *Selitrichodes globulus*

Size: 0.04 inches **Role in Nature:** Herbivore **Discovered in:** a backyard in California

You probably know all about the creatures that live near your house. They may seem kind of boring. But what if they are not? What if there is an undiscovered species in your backyard?

Blue gum gall wasp seen through a scanning electron microscope

ALL GUMMED UP

In a Los Angeles backyard, a blue gum tree was being eaten alive from the inside out! The twigs sagged under the weight of **HUNDREDS OF UNKNOWN INVADERS.** One hundred squirming blue gum gall wasp larvae covered a section of twig only as long as your pinkie!

Gall wasp galls on blue gum tree branches

Blue gum gall wasp larva inside a gall

WELL, GALL-Y

Gall wasps are insects that lay their eggs inside of trees. To do this, a female gall wasp jabs her stinger into a branch, twig, or leaf. The wasp's body pushes her eggs into the hole. The eggs hatch and the larvae, or baby insects, hide inside the tree. The tree swells around the larvae, creating a bump. The bump is called a gall. Galls can turn a tree's smooth skin into **A FIELD OF CRUSTY PIMPLES.**

Inside, the gall is basically a small room filled with the larva's favorite food. The young wasp eats its way out of the gall. **IMAGINE LIVING IN A ROOM MADE ENTIRELY OF PIZZA!** When it is ready, the adult flies away from the gall to lay eggs that make more galls!

500 TIMES ACTUAL SIZE!

UNSOLVED MYSTERY: WORLD TRAVELERS

The blue gum tree is a kind of eucalyptus tree originally from Australia, but it has been planted in parts of the United States. Blue gum gall wasps only eat blue gum trees. The **REALLY WACKY THING** about the blue gum gall wasp is that no one has ever found this wasp in Australia. So far, the wasp has only been found in blue gum trees in Los Angeles, California.

LOS ANGELES

AUSTRALIA

Only 12% of all the creatures on earth have been named. Six million more are waiting to be found. You may think scientists are the only ones making these important discoveries. But discoveries aren't reserved for the experts. **KIDS CAN FIND NEW SPECIES, TOO!** In fact, young people from around the world are doing just that.

To find and officially describe a new species requires skills and determination. It also takes curiosity, close observation, and careful documentation—plus a sense of adventure! **DO YOU HAVE WHAT IT TAKES TO MAKE THE NEXT WILD DISCOVERY?** Wacky creatures may roam just outside your door. . . .

KIDS IN ACTION

T. REX LEECH

Size: 2 inches Role in Nature: Parasite Discovered in: Peru

Scientific Name: Tyrannobdella rex

You might be eager to find a new animal, but not inside your own body, right?! That's just what one nine-year-old did. This girl felt a slithering, sliding sensation inside her nose. Doctors pulled a two-inch leech out of her right nostril! And it turned out to be a new species —the *T. rex* leech!

UP THE NOSE

Three *T. rex* leeches have been found in human noses. The leeches swim in the rivers of the upper Amazon. Some people bathe in these rivers. That's how leeches find themselves **A TASTY MEAL.**

SLURP

A leech latches onto another animal using a sucker-like mouth. It slits the skin, and then **STARTS SUCKING.** That leech might not have to eat again for a month!

SIZE XL

ACTUAL T. REX LEECH TEETH!

Unidentified leech

While some leeches have two jaws, some don't have any jaws at all. The *T. rex* leech is the *only* leech that has one jaw with **EIGHT HUGE TEETH.** Its teeth are five times larger than other leeches' teeth! That's one reason it got the name *T. rex* leech. Plus, the leech's ancestors could have **LIVED IN A *T. REX* DINOSAUR'S NOSE!**

ISABELLA'S BITTERSWEET CLAM

Scientific Name: *Tucetona isabellae*

Size: 0.6 inches **Role in Nature:** Omnivore **Discovered in:** Mexico and California

Teenager Elizabeth Garfinkle never imagined she would write an article that people across the United States (and in other countries, too!) would read. She also never imagined that she would get to name a new kind of animal. But, when Elizabeth officially described Isabella's bittersweet clam, she did just that.

FUN STUFF

Elizabeth's favorite part of the process was getting to name the clam. She chose to name it after Izzy, a two-year-old she babysat. Izzy loved shells so Elizabeth thought Isabella would be the perfect name for "her" clam.

BITTERSWEET BLOOD

Most clams have clear or blue blood. Bittersweet clams have **IRON IN THEIR BLOOD—JUST LIKE PEOPLE.** This makes their blood red!

Isabella's bittersweet clam lives under the sand. Like other clams, it sucks seawater in through a tube. Food in the water sticks to mucus that covers the clam's gills. The food-filled mucus slides into the clam's mouth. **YUM!**

BABY STEPS

When Elizabeth was in the seventh grade, she had volunteered in the laboratory of the Santa Barbara Museum of Natural History. She got to use a scanning electron microscope to take pictures of tiny shells. She did lots of hard work—like taking out the trash and scrubbing shells with a toothbrush. Elizabeth's efforts put her in **THE RIGHT PLACE AT THE RIGHT TIME.** When a curator in charge of the museum realized one of the shells was a new species, he asked Elizabeth to help him officially describe it. The rest is history!

GLOSSARY

ADAPT: To change in order to survive. An animal's behaviors and body parts must be adapted to their environment.

AMPHIBIAN: An animal with a backbone that begins life in the water but lives on land as an adult. Frogs and salamanders are both amphibians.

CAMOUFLAGE: A color, pattern, shape, or behavior that helps an animal blend into the environment.

CARNIVORE: An animal that eats meat. That meat can be from large animals or tiny insects, spiders, etc.

DECAPODA: A group of animals with ten feet and a hard outer skeleton. Crayfish, lobster, and shrimp are all decapods.

DECOMPOSER: A living thing that eats dead plant or animal material.

DNA: A code inside every living thing. An animal's DNA code holds information about its features—like size, hair color, and number of toes.

ENDANGERED: At risk of becoming extinct.

ENDEMIC: Living in only one place in the world, such as one mountain range or forest.

EXTINCT: A species that has died out. It is no longer alive on earth.

FOOD CHAIN: The order in which plants and animals are eaten. For example, grains of grass are eaten by a mouse, the mouse is eaten by a snake, and the snake is eaten by an owl. [See diagram.]

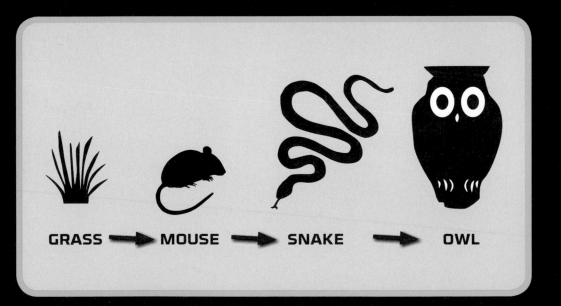

GRASS ➡ MOUSE ➡ SNAKE ➡ OWL

HABITAT: The place in nature where an animal lives. An animal's habitat could be an entire mountain range or a single pond.

HERBIVORE: An animal that eats only plants.

INSECT: An animal with six legs, three body segments, and no backbone.

LARVA: The second stage in the life cycle of some insects. "Larvae" is the word used for more than one larva. Insect life-cycle stages include egg, larva, pupa, and adult. [See diagram.]

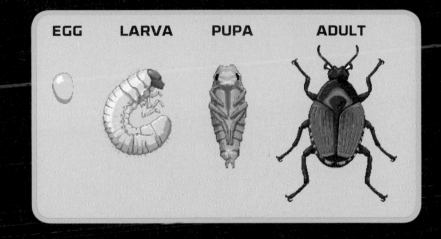

| EGG | LARVA | PUPA | ADULT |

LICHEN: A small organism that usually grows on trees and rocks. Lichen is made up of an algae and a fungus living together.

MAMMAL: An animal that has fur, generates its own heat, and produces milk for its young.

NATURAL RESOURCES: Materials found in nature that are available to be used. For example, water, trees, and rocks are natural resources.

NECTAR: The sweet liquid in flowers that birds and butterflies drink.

NOCTURNAL: An animal that is active at night.

NOSTRIL: An opening in the nose.

OMNIVORE: An animal that eats both plants and other animals.

PARASITE: An animal that lives off of another animal. A parasite may drink the other animal's blood or eat parts of its body, but usually it will not kill it.

PREDATOR: An animal that eats other animals.

PREY: An animal that is hunted and eaten by other animals.

PRIMATE: A group of mammals that includes monkeys, apes, and humans.

REPTILE: An animal that is covered in scales, has a backbone, and does not produce its own heat. Examples: snakes, turtles, and lizards.

SEGMENT: A section of a creature's body.

SPECIES: A group of animals that are all the same type.

SPECIMEN: A single living thing that represents a group of animals.

TRAIT: A characteristic of an animal. For example, zebra traits are stripes, hooves, and the ability to run fast.

ABOUT THE AUTHOR

HEATHER L. MONTGOMERY is crazy about weird stuff in nature—the grosser the better. When she is not catching bugs or checking out an animal skull, she's writing about snake tongues or snail poop. If you want to learn even *more* wacky stuff about these animals or have a question, visit Heather at HeatherLMontgomery.com.

Heather's having a tough time deciding which of the animals in this book is the wackiest. **SHE'D LOVE TO HEAR WHAT YOU THINK!** She might not answer right away, though—she's often deep in a cave, behind a waterfall, or up in a tree.

WITH A ~~LITTLE~~ LOT OF HELP FROM MY FRIENDS

I couldn't have written this book without the help of people who love science as much as I do. Who knows, kids, maybe one day your name will be on a list like this!

Gevork Arakelian, Senior Biologist, Department of Agricultural Commissioner
Bruce Beehler, Naturalist, Conservation International
Bastian Bentlage, Doctoral Student, The University of Kansas
Jason Lee Brown, Postdoctoral Fellow in Biology, Duke University
Carlos D. Camp, Professor of Biology, Piedmont College
Diego F. Cisneros-Heredia, Natural Science Researcher, Universidad San Francisco de Quito
Allen G. Collins, Zoologist and Curator, Smithsonian National Museum of Natural History
Eberhard Curio, Professor and Scientific Advisor, Philippine Endemic Species Conservation Project
Tim Davenport, Country Director, Tanzania Program, Wildlife Conservation Society
Dennis E. Desjardin, Professor and Herbarium Director, San Francisco State University
Henrik Enghoff, Professor and Director of Collections, Natural History Museum of Denmark
Elizabeth Garfinkle, Student, San Roque High School
Jason Gibbs, Postdoctoral Associate, Department of Entomology, Cornell University
William (Bud) Gillan, Honors Biology Teacher, Boynton Beach Community High School
Frank Glaw, Head of Vertebrates, Zoological State Collection of Munich
Frank Hennemann, Collaborator, Rhynchota Section, State Entomological Collections in Munich
Samuel James, Associate Professor of Biology, University of Iowa
Lynn Kimsey, Professor and Director, Bohart Museum of Entomology, University of California Davis
Stefan Merker, Postdoctoral Associate, Goethe University Frankfurt
William M. Moe, Professor of Environmental Engineering, Louisiana State University
Julian Monge-Najera, Director, Journal of Tropical Biology and Conservation, University of Costa Rica
Piotr Naskrecki, Conservation Biologist, Invertebrate Diversity Initiative, Conservation International
Karen J. Osborn, Research Zoologist, Smithsonian Institute
Bill Peterman, Doctoral Student in Biological Sciences, University of Missouri
Anna J. Phillips, Postdoctural Researcher, University of Connecticut
Ted Pietsch, Professor and Curator of Fishes, The Burke Museum of Natural History and Culture
Galen B. Rathbun, Honorary Fellow and Research Associate in Mammalogy, California Academy of Sciences
Daniel Rubinoff, Associate Professor of Entomology, University of Hawai'i at Mānoa.
Mark E. Siddall, Curator and Professor, Division of Invertebrate Zoology, American Museum of Natural History
Christopher A. Taylor, Curator of Crustaceans, Illinois Natural History Survey
Paul Valentich-Scott, Curator of Malacology, Santa Barbara Museum of Natural History
Erik Verheyen, Head of Vertebrate Department, Royal Belgian Institute of Natural Sciences
Robert C. Vrijenhoek, Senior Scientist, Monterey Bay Aquarium Research Institute
William Wade, Professor of Oral Microbiology
Quentin Wheeler, Entomologist, International Institute for Species Exploration

In addition to all those great science folks, I had help from writer friends, too. My fabulous editor, Katie Carella, read and re-read this book to make sure all of the wacky stuff made sense. Plus, I had the help of two great writers' groups.

THANK YOU, EVERYONE!